Memories of Felling

by Anthea Lang

Introduction

This book looks at some of the many 19th and 20th century photographs, many of them reproduced on postcards, which were taken of this comparatively small area. It is not a chronological history of Felling but it attempts to show some of the major events which took place as well as more mundane events. Life here revolved around coal, chemicals, church and council and though there were many changes, the basic focus of many people's lives centred on these and changed with them.

The book is a tribute to Felling people and through a variety of visual images, I have tried to give people today a feel of what life in Felling was all about in days gone by.

I hope you enjoy reading this book as much as I have enjoyed writing it. My thanks are due to George Nairn, Norman Dunn, Jenifer Bell & Maggie Thacker at Gateshead Central Library, Julian Harrop at Beamish, Bob Dixon, Richard Jennings, Roger Fern and of course, my publisher Andrew Clark. It is also a tribute to two previous Felling historians, Joan Hewitt and the late Peter Haywood.

Anthea Lang, November 2015

Previous page: A group of men in their allotment gardens, 1909 – note the pit heaps in the background.

Front cover: Workers (and a boy) at John Pit, Felling, 1890.

First published in 2015, reprinted in 2016 by

Summerhill Books PO Box 1210, Newcastle-upon-Tyne NE99 4AH

www.summerhillbooks.co.uk

email: summerhillbooks@yahoo.co.uk

ISBN: 978-1-906721-98-5

Foreword
by David Almond

Felling's in my blood and bones. It provides the roots of my imagination. My first home was in long-gone mouse-infested White's Buildings by Felling Square. We moved to the Grange Estate, part of the great 50/60s council housing boom. Then back to Felling Square and Godfrey Thomson Court. Then we shifted further up to Coldwell Park Estate. As a boy I walked every day to St John's School by the river. I was an altar boy at St Patrick's.

As I walked and played in Felling's streets, I passed by a sign on the High Street that said ALMOND PRINTER. My Uncle Amos was the last of the Almond printers. I passed by the bookmakers run by my grandfather, John Foster Barber, in Felling Square. I sat in Dragone's, ate their delicious Shilling Specials, and listened to the nattering of my mam, my grandma and their pals.

I played football on the Bankies and on the fields above the town, took intrepid trips into the Heather Hills, which to a boy seemed a thousand miles away from home. From there, my friends and I could see the Cheviots, the North Sea, the coalfields of County Durham, the half built massive ships that lined the Tyne. We heard the calling of larks, the distant din of caulkers in the yards below, the blare of factory sirens.

I spent many peaceful days with my grandfather in his allotment on Windy Ridge. I played scary games of ghosts and monsters in the graveyard at Heworth, and danced around the monument to the Felling Pit Disaster, which contained the names of boys and girls who had been as young and younger than us. It was only as I grew older that I understood that had I been born a hundred years earlier, my fate could well have been the same as theirs. I think that Felling is beautiful. Sometimes I take folk there and I tell them that and they frown. I tell them to look closer, and often they do and they begin to understand, especially when they learn something of its rich history.

This lovely book, with its wealth of photographs and memories, and all those faces gazing at us from the past, will help me to convince them. It helps to show this apparently ordinary town on the slopes above the Tyne, is also a complex and extraordinary place.

David Almond in his younger days in Felling.

David Almond was born in Newcastle and grew up in Felling. He is the author of 'Skellig', 'My Name is Mina' and many other novels, short stories and plays. His work is published in 40 languages and widely adapted for stage and screen.

His major awards include the Carnegie Medal and the Hans Christian Andersen Award. His books 'Counting Stars', 'Clay' and 'Half a Creature From the Sea' are all set in Felling on Tyne.

A Brief History

Felling was originally part of the township of Heworth but its separate history really begins in medieval times when *'a manor at Felling'* was granted to Sir Walter de Selby by the Prior of Durham. In this context, Felling probably derives its name from the actual felling of trees which reflects why today, so many people still refer to it as *'the Felling'*, rather than simply Felling. The manor passed to the Brandling family in 1509 and it is the Brandlings who would have such a great influence on the way in which Felling subsequently developed. However, what the Brandlings really did for Felling was to begin boring for coal. Felling Colliery opened in 1779 and, for the next 150 years, provided a major source of employment in the area.

From the need to transport coal, wagonways and then railways evolved and the Brandlings were entrepreneurial in this respect – although their business sense was perhaps questionable! They bought far more land than they needed for their railways and spent too much on it. Also, as rail passenger services were very new, they were naïve with regard to ticket sales, trusting the ticket collectors to correctly account for the money taken. Within a few years, the Brandling railway had been taken over.

However, despite this, Felling continued to develop throughout the 19th century and three distinct settlement areas arose. These were Felling Shore, Low Felling and High Felling – names which reflect the local topography. Chemical works and shipbuilding concentrated on Felling Shore beside the River Tyne, while Low Felling held the colliery and High Felling the shopping and residential area of town. As might be suggested by the names, the settlements arose largely due to the landscape. From Felling Shore there was a slight rise to the railway line and Collingwood Street and then a much sharper rise which flattened out at Victoria Square, then another rise up Coldwell Street to Windy Nook.

In 1894, the three areas were brought together as Felling Urban District Council but for some years, each continued to be a separate community with its own identity. The Brandling's device, their *'burning brand'*, was used as the emblem for the Council and remained until the Council was merged with Gateshead following local government re-organisation in 1974.

Over the years, Felling has seen many changes. The 19th century saw a huge population rise from 2,887 in 1801 to 24,330 in 1901. This resulted in new streets being built and an expansion in the number of shops. Today, the industries on Felling Shore have largely disappeared, the colliery is now just a distant memory and the shopping centre is currently being re-developed. However, the people of 'the Felling' have come through it all.

The committee responsible for organising the 'old people's trip' from Felling to Whitburn, c. 1904. Robert Sisterson, one of Felling's principal shopkeepers, is on the second row, 3rd from right. Old people's trips were a longstanding feature of Felling life. They seem to have begun in the 1880s and continued until well into the 20th century.

When We Were Young

A group of young children gaze at the photographer and his equipment at Felling Shore. In the background can be seen the chimney of the Zinc Oxide works – children were often never very far away from playing in potentially dangerous situations.

Conditions could be difficult for children growing up in Felling in the early years of the 20th century. Many lived in poverty and early medical reports give ample evidence of children infested with lice, bootless, shoeless and occupying insanitary dwellings. In 1906, there was an appeal for a fund to provide food *'for school children who are unable by reason or lack of food to take full advantage of the education provided for them.'* Many subscriptions were received from workers at the various Co-op branches and groups such as Felling & District Women's Liberal Association. Other subscriptions were offered by teachers and even the scholars themselves.

The first ever medical report carried out in 1909 examined those children who were in their first and last years at Felling schools – altogether 1,209 children were examined and 684 parents and guardians turned out to observe the inspection! Although they were mostly well nourished, the Medical Officer felt

In 1911, there was a national strike of schoolchildren. Felling's local poet J.G. Peters was scathing about it and wrote this satirical poem.

The Striker's Song

Hurrah for the schoolboy strike!
We set all the masters at bay!
We care not a jot for the lessons we've got,
As long as we've plenty of play!
Half-a-day every week we demand;
A penny our standard wage;
So burn your big cause, ere we go back again
We don't care a fig for your rage!

Strike, strike, strike!
We've suffered in silence too long
Down with the cane ere we go back again
So strike! And join the glad throng!

We'll hold meetings in every town,
To inspire the coward and fool;
Our pickets shall wait at the door and the gate
Of every tyrannical school!
Now boys, altogether stand firm;
To each other be honest and true;
With light hearted song the streets we will throng,
And show them what schoolboys can do!

that too many wore too much underclothing. It was not uncommon to find a boy wearing an under-flannel over which he would be wearing two shirts with another flannel square on top of his back and his chest. Indeed, it was still common practice to literally sew a child into his/her undergarments at the start of winter and for them to emerge unwashed and rather warm at the beginning of spring. Sixteen children had the misfortune to be described as '*noticeably verminous*' and many of the girls sporting fashionable long hair were also sporting noticeable nits.

However, some things never change – it was observed that many of the boots and shoes being worn were stylish at the expense of being sturdy. There were annual footwear funds and even in the 1930s there were still concerts being held for these funds at venues such as the Imperia Cinema. Felling Amateur Operatic Society together with various soloists performed at one such concert in March 1932.

Right: Felling Chemical Works School with the feature clock tower,

On 11th August 1845, this rather imposing building was opened for the children of the employees of Felling Chemical Works. It was often referred to as 'Lees School' or 'The Clock School' and was established by Hugh Lee Pattinson, a kindly employer described as '*an ardent friend of education*'. Parents were charged 1d per week to send their child to the school but all books and writing materials were provided. Although Hugh Lee Pattinson did not insist that his employees' children attend his school he hoped that, if not, the parents ensured their children receive some suitable education elsewhere.

Lee's School became one of Felling's best loved schools and later it became the first St John the Baptist RC School. In 1910, the clock, once such a feature of the building (and the works) with its 4' 6" diameter, was removed together with its chimes. A poem about the clock can be found on page 33.

The schools (boys and girls) were situated near the bottom of Brewery Lane. Many children who attended them lived at Felling Shore and had a steep climb up Bank Lane to get there. On their way they had to pass a large chemical waste heap which had been grassed over. Whenever it rained, water seeped through this into a gutter beside the road where it flowed into the Tyne. Due to the stench from the waste heap, the lane was often referred to as '*Stinking Lonnen*'.

Although generally, school reports were favourable, staffing was often an issue particularly in the school's early years. In an inspection report of 1910 it was found that Mary McErlanean, an uncertificated assistant, had charge of the babies class – a class which

St John's RC School Brewery Lane – Here, children at the re-named school, pose with their teacher in 1910.

contained 63 children in the morning and a staggering 81 in the afternoon!

Good comments were frequently received about the conduct of the children. An inspection report of 1910 commented that *'The girls are under refined and gentle influences. They are courteous in demeanour and well trained in habits of cheerfulness.'* The next year, a similar inspection remarked that in the boys school, *'Discipline is well maintained and there is evidence of effective teaching.'*

St John's RC Boys School, 1922 – Standard 7 class with their teacher Cornelius Toberty. Cornelius had the remarkable record of attending the school as pupil, teacher, and deputy head – a period of 62 years.

Left: Here is Cornelius again, front left, this time with the rest of the St John's RC Boys School staff in 1930.

Front row: Mr Toberty, Mr Geraghty, Mr Curry, Miss McStea, Mr Duggan. Back row: Mr Gibbons, Mr Cassidy, Mr Kelly, Mr John Burnett.

Below: St John's RC School, Infant Class, 1922.

Right: Staff of St John's RC Girls School. This photograph was taken during the early years of the Second World War. In 1936, the school had moved from Brewery Lane to Willow Grove nearer the centre of Felling. The new school was built by direct labour.

Back row: Maureen Toberty, Joan Bennett, Margaret Cullen. Front row: May O'Brien, Pat Garvey. Maureen Toberty was the eldest daughter of Cornelius shown on the previous photographs. She did her training at another Felling school, Falla Park.

Above: Holzapfel's Institute and School. This was another school to be linked with an industry. Built in 1909 it was used as an institute and school for workers at the nearby Holzapfel's paint works.

Left: High Felling Council School, 1927.

Stanley Robinson (*right*) is described on the reverse of this postcard as '*Felling's boy soprano*' and performed throughout not just Felling but nationally in the early years of the 20th century. Often to be found performing at meetings of the Felling Brotherhood, he was described in a review of one of their meetings in 1910: '*The soloist, Master Stanley Robinson, sang three solos in an exceedingly pleasant manner*'. The Brotherhood frequently held meetings in the local cinemas and he is also recorded as having sung '*a grand solo*' at the Imperial the same year.

In 1913, Stanley was performing as the entertainment turn at the Corona Cinema where he was described as '*Master Stanley Robinson, the Felling boy soprano, after a tour of many of the principal halls in England & Scotland.*'

Stanley, born in 1894, lived with his parents at 5 Cross Row. His father was a deputy at Felling Colliery and would have been able to secure colliery work for his son. However, at the age of 14, Stanley is described in the 1911 census as vocal, music and picture hall artist. suggesting that he was already doing this professionally.

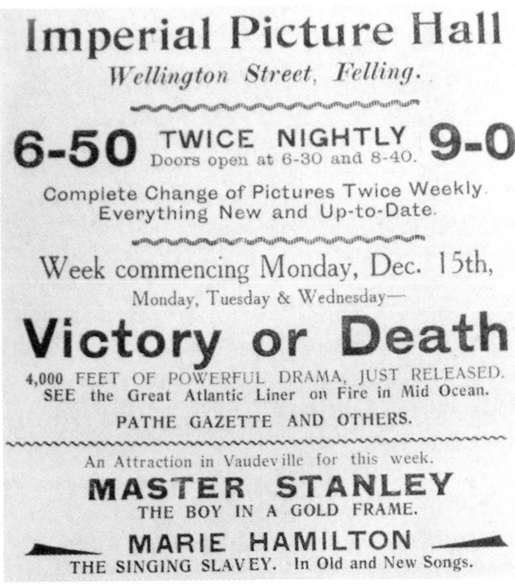

Stanley appearing at the Imperial Picture Hall in December 1913.

Miss Doris Lorraine and her Tiny Tots were a well-known group of entertainers who performed throughout Gateshead during the 1930s. Here, two of them admire themselves in a mirror at Holly Hill Methodist Church.

Felling girl guide troop, c. 1910. Girl guides started as an offshoot of the boy scouts in 1910. Their first uniform consisted of a jersey, worn with a neckerchief. The skirt, knickers and stockings all had to be dark blue and members wore a dark blue cap. In the summer they were allowed to change this for a large straw hat. They also wore a lanyard. Officers wore ordinary 'walking dress' which is what the lady at the centre of the back row is wearing. New troops for both boy scouts and girl guides were formed in Felling during the 1930s.

Children weren't always involved in 'appropriate' activities. When there was a National Unemployed Workers Movement demonstration in Felling in 1938, they soon got in on the act. Communist Councillor Jim Ancrum is on the left near the back.

Juvenile jazz bands became hugely popular in the area in the years following the Second World War. It was every girl's dream to be part of one and huge crowds would turn out to watch the many competitions which took place throughout the North East.

Above: Felling Royals jazz band, formed in 1966, pose for their team photo in 1969.

Left: Children playing on a rocking horse in Felling Park in the 1970s.

Felling Park was a popular venue for children as it contained a children's playground which included swings and what was described as a 'giant's stride', although in common with a number of other parks, for many years these facilities remained firmly locked on Sundays.

HOLY DAYS

For such a comparatively small area, Felling possessed a number of churches and chapels of all sizes and styles and for all denominations. As the years went on, the number of different sects were reduced, as a result of which many buildings were used by a variety of congregations. The Brandling family were staunch Roman Catholics, remaining so even in times of persecution. It was to be some time however, before Felling people got their own Roman Catholic Church. By 1840, there were approximately 400 Catholics living in Felling. Father James Worswick of St Andrew's, Newcastle and his curate, the Rev William Riddell bought the site for a new church on land beside Felling Colliery wagonway from William Caley of Saltwell, Gateshead. On 25th January 1842, a day described as a stormy winter's day, St Patrick's opened. The congregation filled the little church and the first collection taken amounted to £23 18s 4½d. In 1847, the then priest, Father Kelly who had been a joiner prior to becoming a priest (and worked for the whole of his priesthood – 35 years at St Patrick's), added a small presbytery to the church (*right*).

The congregation increased due to the flood of Irish immigrants settling in the area and in 1853 Father Kelly further extended the church and added a gallery. Many of the chemical workers who frequented it on Sundays were still suffering from the effects of a Saturday night's drinking and often exhibited what was described as unruly behaviour – apparently Father Kelly had no hesitation in using '*stronger measures*' when conventional persuasion to behave failed! However, he was a popular priest and the men were happy to work for him even after a full day in the chemical works.

They constructed a school (St John's) which was opened in 1864. But by now, the little church was bulging at the seams as the number of parishioners increased and so Father Kelly began planning a new building. The first piece of earth was turned on 18th April 1872 and the foundation stone laid on St Patrick's Day 1873 in a downpour. Work was progressing well but then, on 11th January 1877, disaster struck when Father Kelly discovered the partially completed building ablaze. By the time aid in the form of hose pipes from the chemical works was received, the building was beyond hope and when the fire was finally extinguished nothing remained but a shell. There was no more building for 15 years and during this period Father Kelly (by then aged 77) retired, too exhausted to continue.

Father Kelly was succeeded by his curate, Father Thomas Caroll who died in 1892 at the early age of 47. He was followed by the Rev John Murphy who, realizing the school was too small, managed to purchase the old Chemical Works School (Lee's School) (*see page 6*) which could take over 600 children.

Father Murphy now turned his attentions to the building of a new church. Plans were drawn up by the Newcastle architect Charles Walker and the Church opened its doors for the first time on St Patrick's Day in 1895. However, '*The first opening was sparsely attended because an admission fee of five shillings was asked. Many parishioners could not afford this and others who could afford it chose to boycott the ceremony on principle. Accordingly a second opening was organized, admission free, this time celebrated by the Bishop of Liverpool.*' This second opening took place on 21st March 1895.

This new church became the glory of Felling with its imposing architecture and beautiful interior. The pulpit stood on a base of Frosterley marble and the windows shown on the photograph below were made by Atkinson Brothers, a Newcastle firm, representing St Patrick receiving his mission to the Irish. They were commissioned by the parishioners in memory of Father Kelly at a cost of £180. The final cost of the building was £13,500 with an additional £1,000 for electric lighting.

Once the new church opened, the old one closed. It was then used as engine sheds for the nearby colliery locomotives and also as a granary. Father Murphy moved to another parish and in 1905 Father Costello began an incumbency which would last 41 years. Like his predecessor, Father Costello further improved the church – he was always regarded as good with budgets and this served him in good stead throughout his time in Felling. For a few years, until his defeat in 1910, he was a Felling Councillor.

Sadly, Father Costello died in 1946 and Father Bernard Stronge then came to the parish. Father Stronge had nearly as long an incumbency as his predecessor as he was the Parish Priest here for nearly 40 years before retiring in 1985. He was a well-known character who received the award of Freedom of Gateshead in the same year in recognition of his services to the area.

However, despite Catholicism's long history in Felling, it was to the Methodists that the honour of building the first religious building in Felling can be given. They held their first services in a private house but in 1811 they built the small chapel (*below left*) at Felling Shore.

St.Patrick's Church, Felling-on-Tyne.

Interior of St Patrick's Church with the font, photographed pre-1912.

Right: Wesleyan Methodist Chapel, situated in Croudace Square, when in use as the Hall of Progress. The little building had a long and varied life. The Wesleyans sold it to the Primitive Methodists in 1830, who in turn sold it to the Methodist New Connexions. It was then sold to the Spiritual Investigation Society who sold it in 1907 when it was re-named the Hall of Progress. As such it was frequently advertised for hire. One notable Methodist preacher here was William Booth who first visited Felling in the late 1850s at a time when he was Minister of the Bethesda Chapel in Gateshead. He would return 50 years later but this time as founder and leader of the Salvation Army.

The Wesleyans meantime built a new chapel on Felling High Street in 1829 (*above right*) eventually moving to new premises at Holly Hill in 1908.

Above: Second Methodist Chapel, c. 1908 when converted to a branch of Walter Willson's stores. A section of their goods entrance can be seen at the left of the photograph.

A Sunday school met in a small vestry attached to the chapel. The vestry was later converted to Mallam's the butchers.

The notice for the foundation stone laying ceremony in 1907 of the new chapel is rather misleading as it advertises that Robert Clayton, Felling's Medical Officer of Health, would lay the foundation stone. He did, but 45 other stones, each individually laid by different people, were also put into position!

This new chapel on Holly Hill was formally opened on 12th February 1908 with an inaugural service followed by a tea and public meeting. Some 800 people partook of tea and, while this was being served, the Dean Primrose orchestra played. After this, a public meeting was held.

A new Sunday school was planned as part of the new Holly Hill Church but was completed nearly ten years earlier and opened 1898. The building was used until the late 1970s when extensive repairs were needed and the congregation moved to the Coldwell Lane Chapel. The Holly Hill premises were demolished in 1976 but were replaced with a new building on Coldwell Street in 1982.

Sunday School, Holly Hill, 1903.

Holly Hill Wesleyan Methodist Church.

The Primitive Methodists, nicknamed 'the Ranters', didn't stay long in the former Wesleyan Chapel on Croudace Row as, in 1833, they bought a piece of land behind the High Street and built a new but small (it could only seat 150 people) chapel for £130 – only £30 of which had been paid when it opened.

By 1864, attendances had outgrown this building and a new chapel was built on Coldwell Street. But even this wasn't big enough for the increasing congregation and so a new, larger chapel was planned to be built next door.

Left: Laying the foundation stones of the new Primitive Methodist Chapel, Coldwell Street. The old chapel can be seen in the background. The new chapel was opened by the Mayoress of Gateshead, Mrs J.T. Scott on 2nd September 1896. It could seat 400 and the whole cost of the building was £1,830 – economical even for those days.

Left: Coldwell Street PM Chapel, 1925. The original church is on the left.

There was school accommodation for 500 children and their teachers. In 1929, the church was extended and a new Sunday school opened at the rear of the premises. The former chapel was then used as a lecture hall but in 1946 was demolished and the site was used as a memorial garden for men who had died in the war.

Coldwell Street Primitive Methodist Chapel was always one of the biggest churches in the Gateshead 1st PM Circuit and, as might have been expected, had a large choir.

Right: Members of Coldwell Street PM Chapel, 1953. The occasion seems have been all too much for the little girl second from the right on the front row.

Sadly, a fire which broke out on Good Friday 1972, caused extensive damage to the building. It could not be saved and for a while the congregation used the former Wesleyan Methodist Chapel at Holly Hill. In 1982, the congregations came together and Felling Methodist Church opened on Coldwell Street, partly paid for by the resultant sale of the Holly Hill Church.

Until Christ Church (*right*) was built, the only Church of England serving Felling was St Mary's at Heworth. Christ Church was founded and furnished by Hugh Lee Pattinson jnr, Robert Robey Redmayne and John Marriner Redmayne and consecrated in April 1866 by the Bishop of Durham, Charles Baring. The church was situated near to the school gates of Lee's Chemical Works School and was built in an early English style using local stone. The architect was R.J. Johnson of Newcastle and four stained glass windows at the west end were gifted by Sir Isaac Lowthian Bell, a noted ironmaster and Liberal politician and Pattinson's brother-in-law.

A Church institute was added in 1885. However, between 1900-04, the foundations were found to have been severely damaged due to colliery subsidence. Once compensation had been claimed and won, a new north aisle was added together with a choir vestry and new incandescent gas lamps. The floors were also re-laid. The architects for these works were Joseph Potts & Son, Sunderland. The church re-opened on 12th March 1906.

Christ Church Boys' Club gymnastic class, 1916. Standing: J. Lynn, S. Knott, J. Brown, O. Winnum, G. Burnet. G. Waltern, J. Charlton, T. Milburn, J. Greenwell and J. Winter. Second row: R. Hadon, A. Sanderson, the Rev A. Simmons, J. Young and E. Creswell. Front row: W. Headlem, H. Mitcheson, T. Taylor, R. Milburn. Reclining: G. Redhead.

Going to church was often about much more than simply religious observance. All kinds of clubs and societies were offered and in the picture above, members of the Boys' Club gymnastics class from Christ Church are shown. Many of these young men were employed on war work at the time the photograph was taken and they are displaying war buttons on their lapels.

CHRIST CHURCH, FELLING.
(Consecrated on April 26th, 1866).

GRAND
JUBILEE TEA
Given by the Ladies of the Congregation, in the CHURCH INSTITUTE,
ON WEDNESDAY, APRIL 26th, 1916,
From 4.30 to 6 p.m.
Adult's Ticket for Tea, One Shilling.

ORGAN RECITAL in CHURCH from 6 to 7.15 p.m.
Service at 7.30 p.m. Preacher:
THE VENERABLE ARCHDEACON OF AUCKLAND
(Formerly Canon Derry, Rector of Gateshead).

SUNDAY, APRIL 30th,
Services: Morning, 10.30; Afternoon, 2.30 (Children); Evening, 6.30.
Preacher at Morning and Evening Services:
REV. F. REDMAYNE, M.A.,
Vicar of Well, Bedale, son of Mr. John Mariner Redmayne, one of the Founders and Patrons of the Church.

The church celebrated its golden jubilee in 1916 and this advert shows details of the grand jubilee tea which was held to mark the occasion. A special guest was the Rev F. Redmayne, son of John Marriner Redmayne, one of the founders.

St Peter's Church – In 1913 Christ Church acquired the former New Connexion Methodist chapel in Wellington Street which they re-designated as St Peter's Mission Church. St Peter's closed in 1948 but until then the church used the title of Christ Church with St Peter's Church. Electric lighting was added to Christ Church as a memorial to those parishioners who had died in the First World War.

Christ Church with St. Peter's Church,
FELLING.
Good Friday:
HOLY COMMUNION, 8 a.m.
MORNING PRAYER and SERMON, 10.30.
"By the Cross," 1.45 to 3 p.m.
Sacred Music: "The Crucifixion," 7.30 p.m.

Easter Day:
HOLY COMMUNION, 6, 7 and 8 a.m.
MORNING PRAYER and HOLY COMMUNION, 10.30.
CHILDREN'S SERVICE, 3 p.m.
EVENSONG and HOLY COMMUNION, 6.30 p.m.
Easter Monday:
HOLY COMMUNION at St. PETER'S, 10 a.m.
Wishing you a Holy and Happy Eastertide.

Right: Easter services at Christ Church in the 1940s.

The Salvation Army began in Felling with the arrival from London on Saturday, 30th March 1878 of two 'Hallelujah lasses' Rachel and Louise Agar. These two held a service on the Sunday and on Monday morning they telegraphed '*500 afternoon; 800 night; Six souls; lot in pickle*' (a '*pickle*' was a standing phrase which meant people were considering converting).

Early meetings were held in the lecture hall over Moses the cobblers at the corner of Coldwell Lane and Crowhall Lane, then later in stables behind Bolam Terrace. They then had premises above a plumber's in Holly Hill. The foundation stones for their first purpose built premises on Croudace Row were laid in May 1904. Nine stones were laid which were declared to be '*well and truly laid to the glory of God and the Salvation Army*'.

Following General Booth's death in 1912, a service was held in the Wesleyan Church on Holly Hill. Members of the Salvation Army who were present wore white armbands as a mark of respect.

In 1928, when times were particularly hard, the Salvation Army ran a soup kitchen and fed literally thousands of children.

A severe fire gutted the Croudace Row building in 1970 and the former premises of the Zion Congregational Church on Smithburn Road was then used.

Right: A Salvation Army wedding of Lily Killen to George F. Shilan in 1939.

Perhaps one of the most informal church groups was the Felling Brotherhood which was formed in 1906, meeting at first in an old cottage in Wellington Street. That had to be demolished to make way for the new Imperial Cinema and so, for a few years, members were allowed to use the cinema for occasional meetings. However, in 1916, the Brotherhood opened a new Institute in Booth Street where they often gave needy children treats on New Year's Day. Advertising for people to join them, they described themselves as '*No long faces, no dry sleepy sermons, no starchiness*'.

LEISURE AND PLEASURE

Felling may have had a selection of Methodist chapels but it held an even greater number of that great enemy to the chapels – the public houses. Large, small, ornate and plain, Felling certainly had a good selection. It also had a popular temperance bar. The following photographs are just a selection of these buildings, some of which are now sadly just a distant memory. A number of these pubs had small brewhouses attached and there was at least one substantial brewery at Felling Shore during the early 19th century.

In 1855, the area of Felling Shore had seven public houses. These would have been well populated by the many chemical workers employed in the area who thought nothing of knocking up a landlord at 6 am in the morning when they had finished their shift. Having inhaled copious amounts of chlorine and bleach, they would have certainly needed their liquid refreshments.

Sunderland Road sported a number of pubs including two named after racehorses. The Blink Bonny (*left*) was named after a filly which won both the Oaks and the Derby in 1857. Situated opposite Felling Park, the building was demolished around 1930.

Right: The Beeswing was built in 1899 for Robert Deuchar, replacing an earlier building of the same name on the same site. It was named after another filly, Beeswing (1833-54) who was regarded as the greatest mare of her day in England. For a brief period in the 1920s the licensee was Tommy Burns, the former world heavyweight boxing champion (1906-08). During his tenancy, he set up a boxing ring in one of the upstairs rooms. The pub was put up for sale in 1919 for £10,500 but remained unsold. Towards the end of its life it was turned into 'Durty Nellie's' – a pseudo-Irish 'character' pub and a sad end to a fine building.

North of the station were these public houses:

Above left: The Wheatsheaf, Carlisle Street – re-built in 1907 for Newcastle Breweries around an earlier building. Although the exterior was modest in size, it was very decorative with its angled top storey window, its decorative 'wheatsheaf' emblem and its smart dark green tiles covering the walls under the name. The first floor was chamfered and so a column was built as a support. However, this frequently caused problems for unwary drunks! The Malting House public house can be seen in the background. *Above right*: Mr Crinnion behind the bar of the Malting House, Carlisle Street in 1930.

Right: Also north of the station was the Mulberry Inn, Mulberry Terrace – seen here in 1950. The Mulberry was formed from the Brandling's home, Felling Hall in the mid-19th century. In 1856, it was advertised for sale '*with a brewhouse capable of 8 barrels*'. It has now been converted into housing.

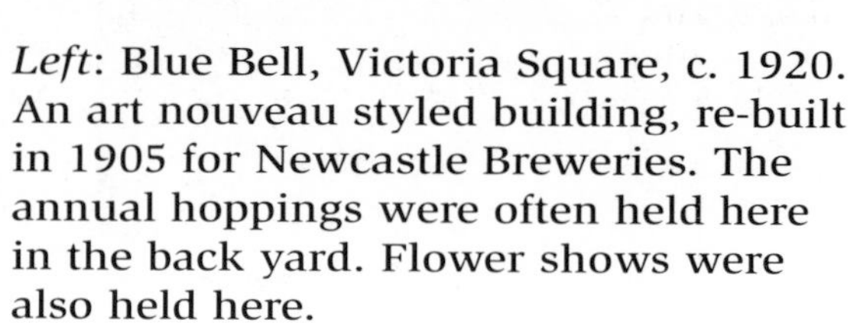

Felling Square (re-named Victoria Square) also contained a good selection of drinking establishments.

Left: Blue Bell, Victoria Square, c. 1920. An art nouveau styled building, re-built in 1905 for Newcastle Breweries. The annual hoppings were often held here in the back yard. Flower shows were also held here.

Right: The Victoria Jubilee public house with the Boer War memorial fountain (the pant) in front, c. 1910. This pub started out life as the Barley Mow but was bought in 1887 and renamed the Victoria Jubilee as a reminder of Queen Victoria's Golden Jubilee which was celebrated the same year.

Drunkenness was often a problem in Felling and a number of groups such as the Independent Order of Good Templars and the Rechabites were formed to combat it. Many towns had temperance bars – public houses which only sold non-alcoholic drinks but the one in Felling had a life longer than most. William Stobbart, described in the 1911 census as a '*bottler of temperance drink*' was a herbalist and confectioner who moved his shop from Victoria Square to Crowhall Lane in 1906. Advertising this, he described himself as '*the sarsaparilla king*'. The building remained a temperance bar until the 1930s by which time it was being run by Ramsays who turned it into a confectioners.

On Felling High Street were two further public houses – the Greyhound and the appropriately named, given its situation, Halfway House.

Stobbart's Temperance Bar in 1910 – otherwise known as 'The Wise Man's Public House'.

Felling had two cinemas. The first was the Imperial which opened on Wellington Street on 7th November 1910. It had seating for 800 and was built on the site of an old cottage which had been used as the Brotherhood Institute. A promise made by the manager at the opening was that performances would be *'free from anything that would tend to lower or degrade'*.

Children's matinees were introduced which proved popular particularly as children were given sweets as treats.

In the early days, the length of film was measured in the length of the film reels rather than the time it took to watch. In 1913, the epic film 'Quo Vadis' was advertised as being 8,000 feet long (it actually ran for two and a half hours – a staggering feat at this time) and was described as '*without doubt, the largest effort yet attempted by the manager*'.

Staff of the Imperial, c. 1914. Although this photograph purports to show the staff in the early days at the Imperial, there certainly seem to be some young recruits!

However, the Imperial was faced with a competitor when a new picture hall opened on Coldwell Street just one year later on 14th November 1911. A competition was held to select a name which was shown on the screen on opening night (*see below*). A prize of £1 was offered – but as there were two winners, the prize was divided. The name chosen was the Corona and, for the next 50 years, there was friendly rivalry between the two although for a short period of time in the 1920s, both cinemas were actually under the management of the same person, Joseph Smith.

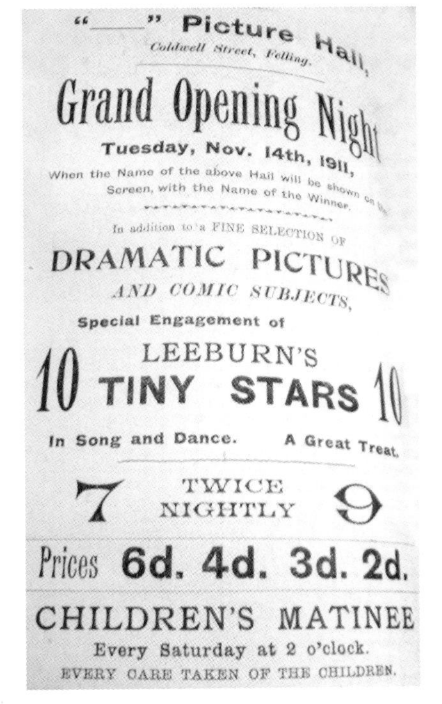

Above: Corona Cinema.

Right: An advert for the picture hall with no name, 10th November 1911.

As with the Imperial, the Corona also offered children's matinees although a bar of chocolate was perhaps more of an incentive than the boiled sweet offered by the Imperial!

The Corona had a heavy emphasis in its early years on exotic sounding stage acts who performed in the intervals while the film reels were being changed. These included Max Merlin, the human crocodile (contortionist), Sim Maree, the india-rubber Mohammedan and Hoo-Ham-Hi, the great illusionist. And, just to add variety, they also had Broncho, the educated horse. The Imperial focussed on more home grown efforts which included the unfortunately named Little Dick who could apparently clog dance on a dinner plate! In 1911 Thalmeda appeared with a big reputation and two tons of scenery. She was famous for her *'living statuary, her classic posing revealing the noblest conception of sculptor and artist'*. Reading between the lines, 'her classic posing' also revealed a fair amount of naked flesh!

Both cinemas were extended within a few years of opening and the Imperial was given a new sign. Unfortunately, it would appear that the letters ordered were too large for the space available with the result that the Imperial became the Imperia for the rest of its life.

On 1st October 1929, disaster struck when the Imperia was gutted by fire. However, within three years, they had opened on a new site, a former dance hall at Holly Hill. This new cinema was without doubt more luxurious than both its predecessor and the Corona. Perhaps the Corona recognised this as it ceased paying for adverts in the 1930s. The Imperia had a new strapline in the 1930s – *'The SUPER-ior House of SUPER-ior Tastes'*. Maybe in keeping with this new, more up-market image, it decided to dispense with the children's matinees although reduced prices for children were available at certain times. As an added attraction, new café coffee dances were held from 1932 which cost 9d every evening. Eventually in December 1935, the hall next door was taken over as the 'New Imperia Assemblage' – which advertised dancing *'on the floor of a 1,000 springs'* with music played by the resident orchestra of Norman Craig and his band. On Tuesdays and Fridays, concessionary prices were available at the first house for those who were unemployed or of pensionable age. It also offered more up-market live entertainment. Well known bandleaders such as Roy Fox and Billy Cotton played here.

Left: Flames shoot out of the Imperia in 1929.

Below: Firemen survey the wreckage.

The Corona in 1956 (shown centre above).

The cinema was also used for other purposes. Ellen Wilkinson, then prospective MP for Jarrow, attended a public meeting at the Imperia in March 1935.

In 1946, a local poll was held to determine whether cinemas should be open on Sundays. Despite an overwhelming majority voting for Sunday opening, J.H. Smith, manager of the Imperia declared that so long as he was in charge, the Imperia would certainly not open on Sundays.

The Imperia remained successful until the 1950s when audiences declined as television took over. The Palais de Dance (the Assemblage) introduced 'Be-Bop' nights on Mondays to try to attract the teenage market but to no avail. The last film shown was 'Voyage to the Bottom of the Sea' starring Walter Pidgeon in 1962. After this, the cinema was converted to a bingo club. In 1982, it was given Grade II heritage status.

The Corona meanwhile had been re-decorated in the 1930s and again in the 1940s but the opposing adverts for both cinemas in the local papers disappeared. To attract a different audience from the Imperia, a heavy emphasis was put on westerns and action films as well as twice weekly children's matinees. In the 1950s, in an attempt to halt the decline of cinema audiences, they began to offer special shows for old people and talent competitions.

The Imperia in 1972.

However, in 1960, the Corona closed its doors for the last time and was subsequently demolished.

Incidentally, not many people realise that Felling had its own Hollywood film star who acted in numerous films in the 1930s and 40s with stars such as Basil Rathbone and Johnny Weismuller. This was Paul Cavanagh although in his Felling days he was known as a popular young school teacher Billy Atkinson. He was a member of Holly Hill church choir and after studying law at Cambridge decided he wanted to be an actor. One of his films, 'Strictly Unconventional' was shown in 1931.

Right: Hoppings, Felling Square, 1900.

The Felling hoppings were a longstanding annual event held at Whitsuntide. During the 19th century, the main attractions were pony racing, old women's races, donkey races, gingerbread stalls and sweet stalls. There was also 'the greasy pole' set in front of the old Blue Bell inn on top of which was tied a leg of mutton or a ham. In 1888 there was a complaint that the size of the fair hindered the Sunday school procession through the square.

By the 20th century, the hoppings were described simply as '*a mere showman's carnival held in a public house yard*'. Following the rebuilding of the Blue Bell, the hoppings were moved in 1908 to the site of what had once been an old carpet factory at the foot of Booth Street, Whilst it was true that some of the original attractions were no longer in existence, there were still plenty to amuse including a roundabout, shuggy boats, coconut shies, an Aunt Sally and shooting galleries. In 1908, the first time the fair had been held outside of the yard, the main attractions were recorded as being a display of Mr Murphy's motor cars and Mr Baker's twin yachts.

By 1913, the hoppings were being described as dying out but they survived until the 1950s. By then they largely comprised fish and chip stalls, ice cream stalls and a few roundabouts and coconut shies. Their location had also moved to Quarry Banks recreation ground.

Right: Watching the band in the park, 1949. Felling Park provided free entertainment for many. As well as amusements for children, the park also had a bowling ground and tennis courts with band concerts being held on Sunday evenings. In 1913, a letter to the local newspaper advocated a visit to the park saying '*A visit to the park … will repay all those who admire the beauties of nature … the tennis courts, and quoit ground are well occupied.*'

In 1952, trees from the middle path were replaced by 25,000 wallflowers and 6,000 tulips on the instructions of Mr T. Foster, the park superintendent. For many years, the park was noted for its beautiful and well-tended appearance.

If people wanted to do more than simply look at plants and flowers, Felling had a number of allotments (*see photograph on title page*). Some of these were already in evidence but there was a big push for more allotments once the First World War had broken out as people were encouraged to grow their own vegetables. Flowers and produce shows were a feature of Felling for many years. Chrysanthemum shows were held in the Lecture Hall of Holly Hill Methodist Church in the 1930s and also in the Blue Bell public house.

Left: Felling flower show, 1923, with Walter Willson's display advertising their baking using Daisy White's quality flour.

Felling had two main football teams – Felling Red Star (*right: c. 1920s*) and Felling AFC who both played at Brandling Park where 3,000 square yards of turf were laid for the purpose. Felling AFC joined the Gateshead & District League in their first season. One of their most successful footballers was Tommy Reynolds, who after leaving the Felling youth team, went on to play for Sunderland and Darlington. Another Felling lad who went on to play in England internationals was Chris Waddle.

Other teams included the Felling Zion Congers, the Felling Odd Fellows and Felling Shore Tyne Villa.

Singing has always been an important part of Felling life and all the churches and chapels had large choirs. In 1919 the Felling Wesleyan Male Voice Party was formed changing their name to the Felling Male Voice Choir the following year. They have competed in many competitions with great success but perhaps their proudest moment was winning the choral competition at the Festival of Britain in 1951.

Felling and District Amateur Operatic and Dramatic Society held their first production, 'The Mikado', at the Corona cinema in October 1923. They disbanded in 1938 anticipating the Second World War but re-formed after the war ended. In 1947, they produced the 'Vagabond King' staged at the Gateshead Empire which was their home until the cinema was demolished in 1966.

Shops and Shopping

The majority of Felling's shops were situated on the High Street which ran steeply downhill (80 feet from top to bottom!) to Sunderland Road – a distance of over 328 yards. However, the majority of people shopping here would have been unaware that this was formerly the site of the great grindstone way, Felling's major wagonway. As Felling's population rapidly expanded during the 19th century, the number of shopkeepers grew.

The variety of shops was extensive and a search of the 1914 trade directory reveals the following list below. Low numbers were at the bottom of the High Street. Even numbers were on the left hand side of the street as you walked down. Not all traders paid for entries in directories, so this is not necessarily representative of every single shop. One of those not listed was number 35 – the furniture shop owned by Ernest Walters. This opened in 1862 and it remained on the High Street for over 100 years

1 G.W. Burnett & Co, confectioner
5 Thomas Heslop, pork butcher
7 Mary S. Wright, tobacconist
11Robert Charlton, butcher
13 London & Newcastle Tea Company
15 James W. Ramsay, watchmaker
19 Ralph Wakefield, butcher
21 James Duffy, fruiterer
27 Walter Willson, grocers
29 River Plate Fresh Meat Company
33 David Bevan, fried fish dealer
37 George Anderson, hairdresser
39 Halfway House (ph)
47 Edward J. Hutchinson, grocer
49 Elijah Copeland, confectioner
55 Charles F. Dornay, pork butcher
57 George Bolam, solicitor
59 Thomas Davis, watchmaker
63 Henry Girling, fried fish dealer
65 John Harrison, fancy repository
67 Robert Arnell, butcher
75 William Nichol, bootmaker
77 James Nelson & sons, butchers
79 Richard Dick, hairdresser
85 William A. Weddle, butcher
89 William Moultrie, hairdresser
91 Robert Nicolson, fruiterer
93 Hawks & Co, confectioners
97 Georgina Dodd, fancy draper
99 M. Galloway, confectioner
101 Gallon's Ltd, grocers

8 William Young, bootmaker
12 Thomas Jewell, butcher
14 John Crosby, baker
20 Robert Smith, newsagent
22 Danish Butter Company
36 James McGuinness, department store
42 Atkinson & Co, drapers
46 Thomas Carruthers, house furnisher
50 Maypole Dairy
52 Lloyds Bank
56 William J. Costelloe, pawnbroker
58 Thomas Dixon, hairdresser
60 Farmers and Cleveland Dairy
62 Duncan & Daglish, beer retailers
68 Elizabeth Little, fruiterer
72 Simon Lang, grocer
74 John Waters, butcher
76 Fred Stuart, manager
78 James Green, cycle dealer
80 John F. Simpson, pharmacist
86 Harry Metcalfe, manager
88 George Hadden, confectioner
92 Thomas Sisterson, pharmacist
94 Robert Sisterson, decorator
102 John Lightfoot, tobacconist
104 George Branch, printer

By the outbreak of the Second World War, many of these shops had changed hands and more recognizable High Street names such as Montague Burton, the tailors (*'the tailor of taste'*), Lipton's, Law's and Maynard's were now trading. Also trading was a firm who still have premises in Felling today – Dragone's ice cream.

Right: Dragone's ice cream parlour at the bottom of Coldwell Street, with the Mechanics Institute on the left. As well as these premises, Dragone's also had their own ice cream van which became a popular attraction on Felling streets.

Guiseppe and Annetta Dragone came to Felling in the 1920s and set up a small shop at 88a High Street. They later moved to Coldwell Street and later still, Crowhall Road. Although they began as ice-cream manufacturers, by the 1950s they were branching out and offering hot snacks at their Coldwell Street premises such as soup, pie and peas, hot dogs and beef burgers.

Right: Felling High Street c. 1925 – Shephard's is top left. Also visible on the left is Almond the printers, the Greyhound public house, the three golden balls of Costelloe's pawnshop and the awning advertising Maypole tea, home of the Maypole Dairy. Towards the bottom centre are the extensive premises of James McGuinness' department stores.

Another shopping family in Felling was the Sistersons who for many years had a chemist's and a wallpaper shop next to each other on the High Street. Robert Sisterson was one of the most recognised (and, incidentally, possibly the most photographed) man in Felling. But their story begins with Robert's father, Thomas, who, while employed at Felling Chemical works, developed an interest in medical herbalism and had some success treating sufferers in the 1853 cholera epidemic. When he was made redundant from the works, he decided to set up his own business in a small shop on the High Street. His window contained a display of sarsaparilla root and dried chamomile flowers and his most notable remedy was that of a 'composition powder' used as a local remedy for colds. This was later developed (but not by him) as Kompo, which became a well known cure sold nationally.

Robert Sisterson (with the bowler hat) and his staff in 1890.

Sisterson's cash drug store.

In 1869, Thomas moved to new premises further up on the opposite side of the High Street. The shop was later taken over by his son Robert who was a painter and decorator. As he wasn't a qualified chemist, he could only sell ready prepared medicines, which is why the store was described as a cash drug store.

However, when his eldest son, Thomas, who was a trained pharmacist, took over in 1911 there was not only a change of name, but also a change in emphasis to a chemist's.

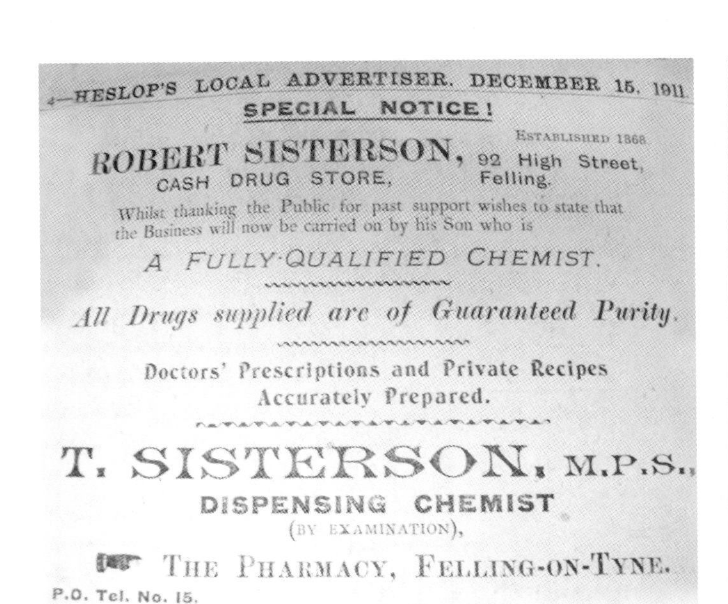
4—HESLOP'S LOCAL ADVERTISER, DECEMBER 15, 1911.

SPECIAL NOTICE!

ROBERT SISTERSON, 92 High Street, Felling.
CASH DRUG STORE,
ESTABLISHED 1868.

Whilst thanking the Public for past support wishes to state that the Business will now be carried on by his Son who is

A FULLY-QUALIFIED CHEMIST.

All Drugs supplied are of Guaranteed Purity.

Doctors' Prescriptions and Private Recipes Accurately Prepared.

T. SISTERSON, M.P.S.,
DISPENSING CHEMIST
(BY EXAMINATION),

THE PHARMACY, FELLING-ON-TYNE.

P.O. Tel. No. 15.

Sisterson's advert, December 1911. Note the early telephone number. By then Robert had opened a second store in 1872, later run by his younger son Stuart, for painting and decorating supplies. The shop celebrated its 50th anniversary in 1922.

Right: Robert Sisterson and son, Stuart, outside his painter's and decorator's shop in 1922.

Robert involved himself in many activities in Felling and became President of Felling's Chamber of Trade.

Chamber of Trade, Felling pictured outside Shanid House, the home of James McGuinness (*see page 27*). Robert Sisterson is seated centre of the front row. When Robert died in 1932, at the age of 82, he was described as Felling's oldest tradesman.

Another of Felling's well known shopkeepers was Emerson Lowes who first managed a shop on the High Street for the London and Newcastle Tea Company until 1915 when he left for war. When he returned he bought Donald Robson's 'working man's' store at 21 High Street and converted the upstairs into a bakery to produce goods for his customers.

Other shops on the High Street included branches of Walter Willson's and Emerson Shephard. Walter Willson's took over the Methodist Chapel on the High Street and converted it into their grocer's premises in 1898 (*see page 12*).

In 1910, Walter Willson's was one of a number of stores damaged in a serious fire which broke out on the High Street and resulted in the complete demolition of Park & Coulson's decorator's shop. The fire brigade had problems putting the fire out as the Council hose was too short to reach the only fire hydrant in Victoria Square and they had to wait for the arrival of the Gateshead fire brigade. As a result of the fire, Walter Willson's held a four day sale of some of their fire damaged stock.

Walter Willson's shop front in the early 1900s.

The same store in 1938.

Emerson Shephard opened a shoe shop at 71 High Street in 1920. This was one of several branches of his main Ellison Street, Gateshead store which he opened after the First World War. He later opened an adjoining drapery store.

Left: Emerson Shephard's store, High Street, 1920.

Felling's first real independent department store, 'Felling House' was owned by James McGuinness and opened in the early 1880s. McGuiness later added pneumatic cash containers to carry the cash from each separate department to one central cashier. After his death in 1907, the business was carried on by his widow Ellen with the help of her two sons, James and Philip. James was killed in the First World War and once Ellen died in 1939, the store closed within months.

McGuinness' store is the large building centre bottom left. At the right of the photograph is Walter Willson's.

The main store of course, in common with many other mining and industrial towns, was the Co-operative Society. Begun as the Felling Industrial Society, this had its origins in a meeting held at Lee's School in 1861. The Society's first shop was opened in leased premises in Neville Street in 1862. However, at a meeting held on 23rd April 1864, it was resolved '*to build a store of our own*'. Situated on Gosforth Street, Sunderland Road, this opened in 1868 and contained not only a grocer's but also included a draper's and a butcher's shop. The building also contained a long room for committee meetings.

Left: The first branch store in Victoria Square. In 1876, the society joined the Co-operative Wholesale Society. This meant that they were now able to buy all their goods from the Society and so did not have to source their own products. For many years, their bread and cakes were supplied by Sunderland Co-op bakeries. The society later opened a branch store in Coldwell Street and, in 1892, they took a five year lease on a shop at the south east corner of Victoria Square. The following year, another decision was taken – this time to buy a pony and butcher's cart.

Right: A young lad poses proudly with the horse and cart belonging to the Co-op butchery department.

Buying a horse could be costly. In 1910, the Co-op paid £64 17s 7d for a new horse and, in 1922, even after they had bought a motor delivery van, they paid £100 for another horse.

The Co-op was always much more than just another shop however. All who shopped there were members and the half-yearly dividend or 'divi' as it was commonly called, was an event eagerly looked forward to. A new store was formally opened at the corner of Crowhall Lane and Windy Nook Lane in June 1898. Members were then given a free tea. In 1902, the Gosforth Street stores were altered when the drapery department moved into what had been the committee room and the grocery store expanded into the drapery's vacated premises.

Right: Felling Co-op's first 'purpose built' store in Gosforth Street. This photograph was taken in 1902 following the alterations described above.

Disaster struck in November 1919, when the Victoria Square premises were severely damaged by a fire which caused several thousand pounds of damage. Due to the prompt arrival on the scene of Gateshead's fire brigade, the butcher's shops and offices were saved but the drapery and provision shops were reduced to a mass of ruins.

New premises on Coldwell Street were planned and while they were being built, the society converted the Royal Lecture Hall, situated above Moses the cobblers at the corner of Coldwell Lane and Crowhall Street, into temporary retail premises.

In 1954, Felling Industrial Society amalgamated with Gateshead Co-op. The Coldwell store was later converted to a 'cash 'n' carry' but closed when the Co-op built a supermarket in the new shopping centre.

Another shopping street in Felling was Gosforth Street (part of Sunderland Road). There were a variety of smaller shops here such as estate agents, chemists, grocers, and Martins Bank which all rubbed shoulders with a good selection of municipal buildings and Felling Park.

For the ever dwindling population occupying the Felling Shore area, a branch of the Felling Shore, Heworth and Bill Quay Co-op was built in Albert Street.

Gosforth Street. The entrance to the park can be seen at the left with the tall dome of the Beeswing public house clearly visible. On the opposite corner to the Beeswing is Barr's grocer's shop.

Co-op stores, Gosforth street, right.

As well as shops, a variety of goods were sold by street hawkers and one of these, Ann Little, became immortalised as 'Cat Nancy' in this ditty:

Two lovely black eyes
Oh, what a surprise,
Only for sellin'
Scotch hares in the Fellin'
Two lovely black eyes

The 'scotch hares' were cats, killed by Ann and substituted for rabbit in the pies she hawked around many of the public houses. She was only caught when the medical officer of health, Dr Kelly, had to investigate an outbreak of gastro-enteritis in the area. When the rabbit pies were found to be the source of the illness, Ann's cellar was searched where cat traps and cat skins were discovered.

Bakers' carts like this belonging to C.W. Burnett, who had their main premises at 1 High Street, would once have been a common sight in Felling.

Farmers & Cleveland Dairy Staff. Fred Maxted, who became the manager, is standing on the cart pictured outside their shop at 60 High Street. During the depression years of the 1930s, some stalwarts of the Felling shopping scene disappeared including the Danish Butter Company, Farmers & Cleveland Dairies, the Maypole Dairy and the British & Argentinian meat company.

Above: Farmers & Cleveland Dairies with Mr & Mrs Armstrong in front.

Right: Of course, no self-respecting area was complete without its post office.

This photograph may have been taken at the opening of the post office on Coldwell Lane in 1909. The first premises opened on Wesley Terrace with a smaller building (originally described as a 'wall' post office) serving Felling Shore. A further post office later opened on Richmond Terrace. In the heyday of postal deliveries, three per day were common in this area.

In the 1970s Felling got a new shopping centre. This was planned as part of what was intended to be a complete transformation of the town centre. The consultants were the firm of J.G.L. Poulson. Its head, John Poulson, was later convicted of bribery and corruption after a major scandal (the long serving Felling Councillor, Andy Cunningham, was also implicated). The plans were revised by the Council architects, Owen Luder and Brian Jones. Phase one provided for 34,000 square feet of shopping facilities which included a supermarket, a public house and several individual shop units while phase two planned to re-site High Street traders in the vicinity of Victoria Square. As a result of this, the High Street was planned to be pedestrianised with land on either side designated for housing developments. However, various difficulties, not least the 'take over' of Felling Council by its larger neighbour Gateshead in 1974, meant that these plans were only partly completed.

Felling's new shopping centre, c. 1974. The Imperia bingo hall can be seen at the rear and Moores stores is on the left. The building at the right was the Co-op store. By the time this photograph was taken, the 'divi' had been replaced by loyalty stamps and membership was no more. Concrete based, the shopping centre lacked the old fashioned charm of buildings it replaced and today is currently being re-developed yet again.

One long established shop which was a victim of the town centre re-development was Moses' boot repairers with its 'Royal Lecture Hall' above. Situated at the corner of Coldwell Road and Crowhall Lane, it was demolished in 1969.

Moses' boot repairers, c. 1920.

Moses' shop under demolition, 1969.

Industrial Life

Industry changed Felling from a largely agricultural landscape to an urban development in the 19th century. The seeds for this had been sown when Ralph Brandling began drift mining in 1670. Nearly 100 years later in 1758, Charles Brandling began boring operations in search of the coal which the family was aware was situated under the surface but which, until then, had been difficult to extract. However, new inventions such as steam engines had changed the situation. The result was Felling Colliery which opened in 1779 and, for over 150 years, provided plentiful employment for Felling's residents. The original seam was closed in 1811 but two other shafts, the John Pit and the William Pit, opened in 1810. In May 1812 disaster struck both pits when an explosion caused by fire damp resulted in the deaths of 92 men and boys (the youngest aged 8) whose names are commemorated on a memorial in the Churchyard of St Mary's Heworth. Out of this disaster, however, came some good as the accident prompted John Hodgson, the rector of Heworth, to demand better safety conditions for miners with the result that the miners' safety lamp was introduced. This was developed separately, but almost simultaneously, by Sir Humphry Davy and George Stephenson.

Despite this improvement however, working conditions could still be dangerous. Further explosions occurred in 1813 (22 lives lost), 1821 (6 dead) and 1847 (6 dead).

John Pit, Felling.

REDUCTION IN PRICES.

FELLING COLLIERY COAL DEPOT.

LOCKELY, COXON & COMPANY.

Price per Cart Load of 15 cwt., and Delivered at the following places.

Class of Coals.	High and Low Felling	Heworth	Heworth and Shore	Felling Shor e	Bill Quay	Windy Nook Lane	New Gateshead
Best Felling Wallsend, Screened - - -	9s 0d	9s 0d	9s 0d	9s 3d	9s 6d	9s 6d	9s 9d
„ „ Unscreened - - -	8s 0d	8s 0d	8s 0d	8s 3d	8s 6d	8s 6d	8s 9d
„ „ Small, 16 cwt. - -	5s 6d	5s 6d	5s 6d	5s 9d	6s 0d	6s 0d	6s 0d

Best Screened at the Depot, from a Stone upwards at 6d. per cwt.
„ Unscreened „ „ „ „ 5d. „
„ Small „ „ „ „ 3d. „

Best Coals in Bags, 3d. each, or 2 Bags for 5½d.
Small „ „ „ 2d. „ „ 3 „ „ 5½d.

Applications to be made at the Colliery to HENRY COXON or JOHN WH[illegible]

Left: Coal prices in 1879. Wagonways transported the coal to staithes at Felling Shore, close to an area known as the Goose Bank. One of these wagonways was known as the Great Grindstone Way. This was seven miles long and ran from Washington through Leam Lane and Windy Nook before ending at the staithes. Part of its route ran down what would later be Felling High Street.

The staithes were originally built of wood but later replaced by iron. Using staithes meant that coal could be easily loaded on to the collier ships. The men who did this job, the teamers and trimmers were well paid as their work could be fraught with danger. The teamers had the job of ensuring that there was no blockage in the chutes down which coal was delivered from the coal trucks on the wagonway onto the ship below. The trimmers work was regarded as even more dangerous as they had to ensure that coal was evenly distributed in the hold of the ship.

The 'Reine Elisabeth' possibly a Belgian collier, moored at the staithes in 1925.

Felling Colliery officials, 1890. The gentleman wearing the top hat is Dr Kelly, Felling's Medical Officer of Health.

The colliery had its own St John Ambulance brigade. In 1907 they were recorded as having 89 members and about 132 certified men in the colliery. This was approximately 16% of the total workforce which was regarded as a high proportion. The colliery provided a horse ambulance and this proved extremely useful at the Felling Rail disaster (*see page 41*).

The colliery also had a band which was formed in February 1900. Over the next 10 years, they won 117 prizes. Their bandmaster was James Oliver.

Coal continued to be produced in Felling until May 1931 with boom years immediately before and during the First World War when over 1,000 men were employed at the colliery.

But it was later industries, such as quarrying and particularly the chemical works, which had the greatest effect on the landscape.

The first major chemical works were opened in 1834 on a 17 acre site by John Lee and his nephew Hugh Lee Pattinson on land to the east of Brewery Lane at Felling Shore.

Felling Colliery St John Ambulance – This continued after the colliery closed.

Left: John Lee's Chemical Works, Brewery Lane, Felling. This is an early daguerreotype and it was probably taken by Hugh Lee Pattinson – a very keen early photographer. When the main chimney (170 feet high) was demolished in 1908, it needed 11 charges of gelatine to blow it up.

The works at its height employed 1,400 people. As well as the buildings directly associated with the chemical works there was also an iron works which made wagons for the works' own railway which ran in a tunnel to their own quay at Felling Shore. The firm also made their own bricks using a disused brick works on their site. One of their main products was sulphate of ammonia – a process devised by Hugh Lee Pattinson as a substitute for white lead – which was exhibited at the Crystal Palace in 1851. Other products included soda crystals, caustic soda, bleach and Epsom Salts.

The owners were paternalistic and looked after their employees. During the 1849 cholera epidemic hot baths were made available for the workers for a small charge due to '*the difficulties in small dwellings of encouraging personal cleanliness which is so valuable an aid to healthy life*'.

The closure of the works in 1886 caused great hardship to many in Felling. The premises were extensive and a major landmark on the 1st Ordnance Survey map produced around 1858. By the second edition, produced 40 years later, the area was bare.

However, there were other smaller chemical works situated near to Felling Shore and further west to Gateshead. These all emitted noxious fumes and vapours – no matter how high their chimneys were built. Those people who lived in the streets around Brewery Lane had to exist in what must have been a fairly eye watering environment. Towards the end of the 19th century, production improvements led to the relocation of much of the chemical industry to Teesside.

Long after the factory had closed its doors for the last time, people still fondly remembered the sound of the men's clogs as they ran down the street when the factory bell sounded and memories even prompted this poem, re-printed in the local press in 1908.

Lee's Factory Bell (anonymous)

The old, familiar factory bell,
Whose resonant clamour we know so well
Is silent now, and its warning clear
Will fall no more on the listening ear.
In youth we heard it, in manhood's prime
It told us still of the flight of time.
In friendly fashion it seemed to say
'The hours are rapidly passing away,
Work with energy while you can,
For few are the years in the life of man'
The rousing message we heard of yore
And learned to love we shall hear no more,
And sad is the heart as it bids farewell
To the vigorous voice of Lee's factory bell

The prominent civil engineering contractor, Walter Scott, who had many business interests, took over much of this area in 1897. One of the things he acquired was a printing works, which led him to set up as a book publisher. The Walter Scott publishing company produced many literature 'classics' from their Felling-on-Tyne premises although printing here had ceased by the 1930s.

Right: Felling Zinc Oxide Co, Felling Shore. There was a brief resurgence of the chemical industry at Felling Shore when the Zinc Oxide Company (Zinc Oxide was used as a soothing ointment for skin irritations) took over Gallon's disused paper mill in 1910. The paper mill was an early industry here, originally owned by Thomas Lightfoot. In 1835 it burned down (paper mills were notorious for catching fire) and was later rebuilt. In 1876, while under Thomas Gallon's ownership, a huge explosion caused the deaths of five men.

The building on the left of the image, surrounded by a wall was the house used for the Felling Shore's Co-op storeman and the steps at the extreme left were always known as the 'clarty stairs'. The chimney shown here dated back to the paper mill days.

Other industries which had disappeared by the 20th century at Felling Shore included a firebrick works, a copperas works and a forge. Richard Wellington Hodgson, who became Mayor of Gateshead, produced grindstones here. Quays were also a feature of this area and boatbuilding was carried out. However, as the 20th century dawned, and bigger berths were needed to accommodate the larger ships, the quays on Felling Shore could not be extended and so that industry too declined.

Employees of International Paints in the 1920s.

International Paints staff, 9th November 1955.

New industrialists included Holzapfel's and Noble and Lund. Max and Albert Holzapfel came to England from Northern Germany in the 19th century and established paint works in Newcastle specializing in marine coatings for ships, then came across to Gateshead and established a paint works there. They expanded, then in 1904 opened even larger premises in Felling. By this time they already had other factories in Europe but the Felling factory was their landmark factory. By the outbreak of the First World War, they had changed their name to International Paints. Today, the Felling factory is still International Paints' largest industrial premises and their company's registered address.

Harry Noble and Pearson Lund founded the Northern Machine Tool Works in Newcastle in 1886 but moved to Felling in 1893, using some of the former chemical works buildings. By the outbreak of the First World War they were specialising in lathes, drilling machines and machine tools and at their peak employed over 500 workers. The business closed in 1998, reforming just three years later.

Right: Employees of Noble & Lund, 1949.

Felling had begun as an agricultural settlement and, although largely replaced by the coal and chemical industries as major employers, farms lingered here until the mid-20th century with Crowhall, Bog House and Grange farms still being farmed by John Rowe, and Felling farm run by Edward Black, at the start of the First World War. By the beginning of the Second World War, only Grange farm remained, worked by Rowe's son Frederick. Both Bog House and Crowhall farm lands had by then been given over to new housing estates.

Many of Felling's early houses were stone built and there were numerous sandstone quarries in the area which were eventually built over – one of these quarries was subsequently landscaped to form Felling Park.

The 1930s saw a rise in unemployment and marches were frequently seen in Felling, often organised by the National Unemployed Workers Movement. One of the leaders in Felling was the Communist Councillor, Jim Ancrum. An Employment Exchange ('the dole') opened in 1936 in Holly Hill, replacing an earlier building on the High Street. The building is interesting for having on its façade a stone with the royal cipher of Edward VIII, who abdicated in 1936 – a rarity due to his short reign.

Eventually, the lack of employment in Felling led to its designation as a 'dormitory town' for other areas.

Bricks and Mortar

Brandling Station

The Brandling Junction Railway began running in 1839 on a line which originally ran from Oakwellgate station in Gateshead, across Felling and Heworth to Brockley Whins and then branched off to South Shields and Monkwearmouth. A little station was built at Felling but it was so small that it could only seat two to three people. Consequently, the larger (but still small) station shown right was constructed in 1842. It was built in a much more ornate style than might have been expected for such a comparatively minor station but as the railway cut through the grounds of Felling Hall, Robert Brandling directed that it should be decorated in keeping with its relatively grand surroundings. In the photograph, the arms of the Brandling family can be seen above the windows.

The building remained in use until 1896 when the line was doubled to four tracks and a new island platform station was ceremonially opened, with music being performed by Heworth Brass Band. The older station was then used for a time as a stable. Today, Brandling station is one of the oldest railway stations still in existence.

Mechanics Institute, Coldwell Street

The Mechanics Institute was built on Coldwell Street and replaced an earlier building on the same site. The foundation stone was laid by Alderman John Lucas of Gateshead Council, a prime mover in the field of education, on 18th February 1892 and formally opened by Sir Charles Mark Palmer seven months later.

The building cost £1,300 and was designed as a two storey building built of local sandstone by Henry Miller, Felling's Council Surveyor. Robert Sisterson provided the interior decoration and the building contained a billiard room, reading room, library, smoke room, club room and lavatories. In 1910, further improvements were made, largely financed by a few male members paying 6d for the privilege of having tea in the company of the ladies at their weekly meetings. This was obviously something quite out of the ordinary as the teas were later described as *'events ever to be remembered'.*

The Mechanics Institute later became a billiards club.

Felling Council Offices

This magnificent building on Sunderland Road was also designed by Felling's Surveyor, Henry Miller, and opened in 1902. It was built of local sandstone and contained a 24 seat council chamber. It is now a Grade II listed building. The opening is described on page 40. It was used as premises for the Medical Officer of Health and also the Relieving Officer and for a few years was used as the Registrar's premises. Miller also designed a 'state of the art' refuse destructor which opened in 1906 as well as designing the park and the pant.

The Boer War Memorial – 'The Pant'

The pant (*seen on the right in 1920*) was unveiled in 1904 (*see page 41*) but within three years there were complaints '*that the trough is not kept as clean and as free from stones as it might be*'. However, the structure was popular, frequently providing a meeting point and there was a public outcry when it was removed in 1952 to make way for the re-development of Victoria Square. The official version was that the pant was a danger to pedestrians and vehicles passing through Victoria Square but there were many protests and despite promises by Felling Council that it would be re-sited elsewhere, it never was and was eventually broken up.

Houses and Homes

Housing in Felling originally centred around the Felling Shore area, consisting mainly of stone built houses. Stone was never a problem to find in Felling as there were a number of quarries in the area. By the 1st edition of the Ordnance Survey map there was housing at both Low Felling and High Felling although the latter only extended slightly south of Victoria Square with only Coldwell House and the Parsonage shown on Coldwell Street.

The largest house in Felling Shore was Nest House, for many years the home of the colliery owner, Thomas Easton and his family. His daughter, Emily Matilda, continued to live in the house until she died aged 95 in 1913 by which time she was a millionairess. A later occupant was her nephew, Henry Cawood Embleton, also a colliery owner, who was president of both the Newcastle and Gateshead Choral Union and also the Leeds Choral Society. While he was living here, a frequent visitor to the house was his friend, the composer Sir Edward Elgar. The house took its name from its situation near what was once known as the Hawk's Nest.

Felling Lodge, Collingwood Street. This house was built at Low Felling in 1827 by the surgeon, Mr Lammas and was later occupied by the manager of Felling Colliery. For many years, it was the home of Felling's doctors – Doctors Kelly, Miller and Cosgrove. In front of the Lodge, a dip in the road marked the course of the Blackburn which had to be culverted when the new turnpike, Sunderland Road, was laid in 1796. The Blackburn marked the original boundary between the former manors of Felling and Heworth.

Crow Hall, c. 1900, with cottage on the left. This is probably Felling's oldest grand house, dating back to at least 1750 although the cottage may date to 1710. The house belonged to the Dean and Chapter of Durham until it was bought by two Felling men, John Thompson and William Rowell in 1893. It gained its name from the crows which nested in the surrounding trees. It was situated on Sunderland Lane, which, as its name suggests, was the first 'main road' to Sunderland. When Sunderland Road was opened in 1796, Sunderland Lane was re-named Crowhall Lane after this house.

Crowhall Cottages, 1970. This photograph was taken when the then owner was carrying our extensive (and expensive) renovations on the property.

Holly Villa, c. 1973. Holly Villa was built in 1859 by W.M. Brown, the owner of both Heworth Burn (where the finest 'blue stone' was produced) and Crow Hall Quarries.

Shanid House (*see page 25*) at the end of Crowhall Lane was the home of shop owner James McGuinness and his family. Jane Toberty, their servant in 1901, was the elder sister of the schoolteacher Cornelius Toberty shown on page 7. McGuiness' profitable department store on Felling High Street provided the money to finance the house which was named after a castle in County Limerick, Ireland where his wife Ellen came from.

It wasn't always easy for a stranger to find a particular address – in 1910, in anticipation of the following year's census, it was decided to erect street names '*where necessary*'.

Felling Shore Housing

For those not fortunate enough to live in large houses with their own grounds, conditions could be difficult. The image right shows how the many workers packed into the Felling Shore area towards the end of the 19th century had to live. These houses were squeezed in around the paper mill and other factories with the distinctly unsavoury smell of neighbouring chemical works permeating the atmosphere.

People not occupied in Felling Shore industries however, soon began to move further uphill to Low Felling where houses were built behind the railway line in streets such as Mulberry Terrace and Brandling Street, and High Felling where housing developed around the High Street with some intermittent development up Coldwell Street by the 1890s.

Left: Uxbridge and Stewart Terraces in Low Felling. A mix of children are posed here – some with smart collars, others with no shoes.

These streets were largely occupied by salaried workers such as teachers and clerks and were built in the 1890s. In the same area, Asher Street and Tulip Street had been built by 1919 and Fenwick, Elsdon and George Streets were all built alongside the former William Pit off Sunderland Road.

At High Felling, a nearby grass field, shown as 'the holly hill' on the 1766 enclosure map, later gave its name to the street Holly Hill. In 1843, on a map prepared by the surveyor John Bell, it is simply called '*the lane leading from the High Felling to the Low Felling*'. It was originally regarded as a hamlet rather than a street, with most house building here taking place at the end of the 19th and beginning of the 20th centuries, although substantial houses such as Holly Hill House and Holly Hill Villa were built earlier as was a poorhouse in 1821. The houses were built in a mix of styles with those shown above right rather more substantial than the rest.

Further housebuilding continued in the High Felling area up to the outbreak of the First World War and by 1914, Coldwell Street (which connected Felling with Windy Nook) was presenting a much more 'joined up' appearance. Hewitson and Woodland Terraces (off Coldwell Street) were built and Park Road changed its name to Falla Park Road.

New housing at Holly Hill, c. 1905.

Coldwell Street got its name from the 'cold well' which was once a source of fresh water for local residents.

Two views of Chilside Road – in the 1930s (*above*) and the 1950s (*below*). It wasn't long before the saplings shown in the 1930s had grown to substantial trees twenty years later.

In the inter-war years of the 20th century, Felling's housing was transformed as new council houses were built to rehouse many people who needed to be re-homed following an extensive slum clearance programme (largely financed by government loans). First to be built was the prestigious 'garden city' influenced Watermill Lane estate. Built on the former Bog House farm, these houses were built with Tudor style facades on curved streets landscaped with trees.

By 1938 over half of Felling's population was living in Council houses. The Council's success was recognised by Manchester and Salford Better Housing Council who visited in 1932 and wrote that '*Felling Council had built some very good houses and were letting them at reasonable rents*'.

Another estate was Nest House, built on farmland south of the former Nest House. The land was bought in 1932 but couldn't be developed until the farmer's lease on it ran out in 1934. Felling's 2,000th council house was formally opened here on 18th June 1938. The house was three bedroomed with an inside bathroom and WC, lit by electricity and had large front and back gardens. It was furnished, free of charge, by Mr E. Walters, who had a furnishing shop on Felling High Street. This estate was later completely cut in two when the Felling bypass was constructed in 1959. The old housing in and around Brewery Lane at Felling Shore disappeared and was replaced by the Felling House estate (also known as the Brandling Estate) where 125 houses were planned capable of housing 550 people.

However, not all planned slum clearances were straightforward. In 1935, a housing enquiry had to be held regarding the proposed demolition of houses in Crowhall Lane, Coldwell Street and Garden Terrace with many owners upset that their homes were to be demolished rather than improved. A number of these property owners were represented at the enquiry by the Communist Councillor, James Ancrum. In 1936, new houses were built behind Falla Park School and new private houses were built at Coldwell Park Drive off Coldwell Street. All these new houses needed new furniture and in 1938, an 'Ideal Home' exhibition was held at Christ Church. Residents of the new council estates had their own tenants association and began holding annual trips to places such as Rothbury and the Lake District. They also organised 'field days' for children.

After the Second World War, temporary houses were built at Carlisle Street, Balmoral Terrace and The Drive, although a shortage of building materials caused severe delays. Council house tenants were urged to plant more vegetables in their gardens and in an attempt to improve the neglected appearance of many of the gardens, a competition was held for the best one. The winner received £10 and a shield. Felling Park provided a ready supply of plants for tenants to buy for their gardens and allotments.

Some council houses were allocated to police officers who received an allowance as part of their salary to pay the rent. However, there was fierce competition among other people for these new houses and suspicions of favouritism and queue jumping resulted, as this little poem printed in 'The Felling News' in 1949 shows:

There was a young man from the Felling,
With his wife went in search of a dwelling.
Yes, he got one that's true,
But between me and you
How he got it – ah, that would be telling!

Maps of the 1950s were still showing the 'old' areas of Felling Shore, Low Felling and High Felling although by then, there were few residents living in Felling Shore, while Low Felling and High Felling had merged in most people's minds to become simply 'the Felling'. Crowhall Towers which opened in 1970 was Felling's first block of high rise flats, and was built on the site of the former Methodist Free Church. Also on the same site was built a health centre and St Oswald's Court. These were all part of the new town development.

Another high rise block of flats was Balmoral Drive. These flats had a short life and were demolished on 12th July 1987 (*below*).

Times To Remember

There were a variety of short lived Felling newspapers produced during the 19th century but none of these made it to the 20th century. However, an alternative to the printed word was the town crier (the 'bellman' in the North East) who, as well as relaying the burning issues of the day, earned extra money by going from street to street giving reports of lost children.

Mike the Bellman, c. 1890.

Caxton House – home of Heslop's Local Advertiser.

The gentleman pictured above is Michael Pearson, affectionately known as 'Mike the Bellman' who was blind. For half a crown he would parade around Felling ringing his bell three times in every street and crying out the names and descriptions of children who had strayed from home. He lived in Colliery Row, Low Felling and was often accompanied by his niece who would help him safely manoeuvre the streets.

The end of the 19th century saw the introduction of Felling's (later re-named Heslop's) Local Advertiser which was produced until the mid 1950s. As well as local news articles, it also contained plenty of adverts for all manner of goods, services and events. The premises (the aptly named Caxton House) were built beside St Patrick's Church and are still there today although converted to houses.

New Council Offices, 1902

Felling Urban District Council was formed in 1894, bringing together the previously separate villages of Felling Shore, Low Felling and High Felling. The new Council needed a substantial building as befitted their new status and Henry Miller, Felling's first Council Surveyor, was tasked with the design, Miller was responsible for a number of buildings in Felling but this was architecturally regarded as his finest.

Right: Laying the foundation stone of the new Council offices in 1902. Robert Sisterson can be seen fourth from the right, first row. Henry Miller is at the centre of the photograph back row to the right of the stone.

South African War Memorial, 1904

Right: The opening ceremony of the South African War memorial – 'the pant'. This memorial to the South African War (1899-1902) was unveiled at 3 pm on 4th June 1904 by Colonel Woodland in front of some of the men who had served in the campaign together with the Felling Company of the 8th DLI, accompanied by the band of the 5th DLI. It was erected by public subscription, with every working man contributing one shilling to the memorial fund. It cost £140 and was carved out of Heworth Blue stone. Newcastle and Gateshead Gas Company gave artistic lamp pillars which were placed at each corner. The pant was 18 feet high and on one side was a granite bowl for public use and, on the other, a combined horse and dog trough. It was designed by Henry Miller, the Council Surveyor, who prepared all the preliminary drawings free of charge. Accepting the pant on behalf of Felling UDC, Councillor Major said that he accepted the fountain with pleasure and promised that it would be kept in good order and condition and he would ensure *'a constant supply of water for man and beast'*.

'Leeds Express Smashed', 26th March 1907

The wreckage of the Leeds to Newcastle express.

Work begins on removing the engine and carriages.

This was the newspaper headlines when this accident was reported in the 'Daily Chronicle' on 27th March 1907. It took place the day before, at about 1.40 pm – just 10 minutes before the 10.52 am Leeds express to Newcastle (nicknamed 'the White Express' due to the colour of its carriages) was due to arrive at Newcastle Central Station using the Leamside loop line. Surprisingly, this wasn't an accident due to mechanical problems but was caused by unseasonal weather. A sharp overnight frost had been quickly followed by an unusual heat wave which caused the lines to expand and kink. A temperature of 65 degrees was recorded but at the section where the line buckled, the temperature was estimated at 85 degrees. In summer, the bolts in the rails would have been adjusted accordingly but it was not thought necessary to do this at this time of year.

The accident took place behind the Blink Bonny public house and considerable damage was caused. The guards van was completely shattered and the first carriage was a total wreck. Not surprisingly, this was where most of the injured were to be found. Of the eight carriages, all but two were completely derailed. One carriage was completely divided by a rail thrust through the floor, breaking through the carriage roof.

Doctors, Felling Colliery ambulance brigade and police constables were soon on the scene. Windows had been shattered and some of the train doors were flung into adjoining fields.

Eight passengers were seriously injured, two of whom later died. At the subsequent inquest, the signalman, Charles Anderson, was exonerated from all blame.

Right: Officials arrive to investigate the accident.

Visit of General Booth, 1908

On 1st July 1908, William Booth, General of the Salvation Army and by then a very old man, visited Felling. Outside the pant was displayed a 'Welcome to our general' sign and flags and bunting were displayed throughout Victoria Square.

Felling Park Opens, 1910

The construction of Felling Park was quite an achievement. It was built on the site of a former quarry and was difficult to plan as it covered a number of different levels. It covered two acres and included a children's playground and tennis courts, with a bowling green added later.

Left: Felling Park with the Council offices behind.

The park opened on 27th July 1910. Proceedings began in Victoria Square where Felling Colliery prize band played from 6.45 pm. They then processed and played again at the main entrance to the park on Holly Hill where the Chairman of Felling Council, W. Taylor JP, formally opened the park. The Council provided £2,250 together with a further £250 for the land out of council revenue.

First Aeroplanes Seen Over Felling, 1911

High excitement was seen in Felling on 24th July 1911 when crowds gathered on the Quarry Banks waiting to see their first aeroplanes. The French pilot, Jules Vedrines and his plane appeared first, closely followed by a second plane with 'Beaumont' (real name Jean Louis Conneau) second. After a few minutes, a third plane was spotted. All were taking part in the Daily Mail £10,000 Circuit of Britain flying race. The local historian, John Oxberry, recorded that '*In the near future, the passing of an aeroplane or two over the district may call for merely a passing remark*'. However, this was the first time planes had flown over Felling and resulted in a

Jean Louis Conneau aka 'Beaumont'.

walkout of the apprentices at Noble & Lund's who all 'knocked off' at breakfast time to watch for the aeroplanes. They could be seen occupying the top of the hill and cheering as the planes passed overhead.

The perils of air travel were apparent in this race – out of 30 entrants, only four completed the 1,000 mile course!

The First World War

Almost within a week of the First World War being declared, a war distress fund had been established in Felling and in September an advert for a temporary clerk for the committee was advertised at 35 shillings per week. Within a few months, the fund had reached four figures. Colonial gifts of flour, cheese and potatoes were distributed by the Co-op and the North Eastern Railway Company. But it wasn't long before shopkeepers began using the war as a way to advertise their goods. The Co-op became particularly adept with their slogans many of which had war time references.

Real Scotch Shortbread
FOR
SCOTS ABROAD.
Orders for the Mails now being booked.
CROSBY'S 14 HIGH STREET, and WALLIS STREET, Felling.

Above: Crosby's advert appealed to relatives of the many Felling men who joined the Tyneside Scottish Battalions of the Northumberland Fusiliers.

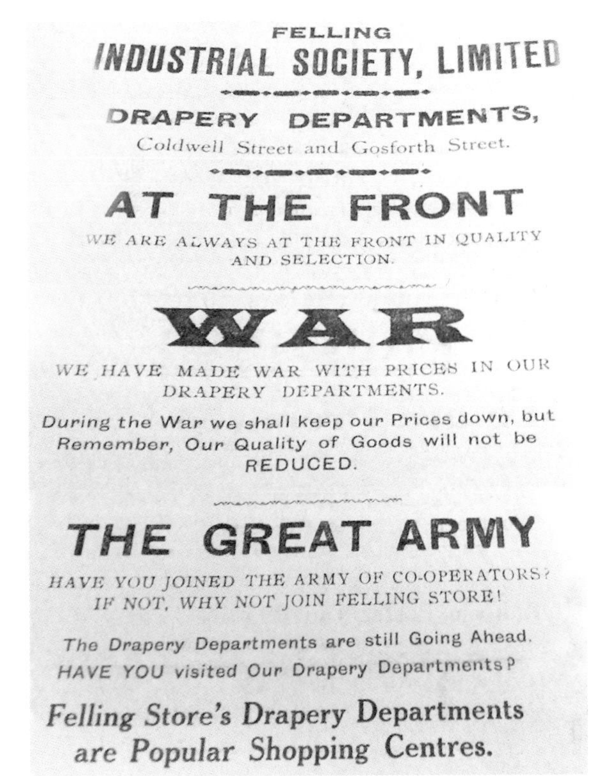

Right: The Co-op '*At the front in quality and selection*'.

The ground floor of Felling Council offices was used as a recruiting office.

The First World War was a boom time for Felling's industries and the colliery reached its peak of production employing 1,065 men.

Many local women joined the Felling Women's Working party formed in 1915. They sent many gifts to France but they also sent socks, mittens, mufflers, shirts and night shirts to Armstrong College Military Hospital in Newcastle. As the war progressed they began to visit the patients and baked cakes for them. Their flag day on 10th June 1916 raised £53 5s 10d.

Another initiative raised £40 for the Army Christmas Pudding campaign – this money was enough to supply a pudding large enough to supply an infantry battalion (about 1,000 men)!

Social events for wounded soldiers at home were organised at the Mechanics Institute. 137 members of the Institute served in the war of whom 21 died and, in 1920, a roll of honour was unveiled to their memory.

Battle of the Somme, 1916

In September 1916, both of Felling's cinemas were showing 'The Battle of the Somme'. This was the first authorised footage of the First World War to be shown publicly. Although some of the scenes were staged, this film showed for the first time some of the savagery of war and the terrible conditions in which men were fighting. Described as '*real war in all its glory*', the film had a profound effect on those watching it.

Royal Visit, 28th July 1936

The Duke and Duchess of York (later King George VI and Queen Elizabeth) arrived in Felling to inspect the Women's Community Centre where they stayed for about half an hour. The Duchess was a Patroness of the Toc H League of Women Helpers who had provided the money for the centre.

The Second World War

Plans for the Second World War were already underway in 1938. There was a report that trenches were to be dug in Felling Park and adverts for men to join both the Auxiliary Fire Service (AFS) and to be Air Raid Precautions wardens appeared in the local papers.

The AFS required men to be fit and over the age of 25. They were called to their first fire, discovered in an uninhabited house beside the Blink Bonny public house, on 1st December 1939 and their second was to a fire at the Duke of Cumberland public house on 6th January the following year.

Felling AFS outside Dempsterville, Low Felling, c. 1940. The commandant of the AFS was Councillor W.S. Greenhall and the section officer was Mr S. Walters.

Public air raid shelters were erected throughout Felling although they were rarely needed. The largest of these could house 200 people. Two people were injured after a small number of incendiary bombs were dropped at the Coldwell Park estate on 15th August 1941. In December that year, two high explosives fell in open ground but caused no injuries or damage and on 12th March 1943, there was superficial damage to some houses at Felling Shore from a bomb dropped at the other side of the River Tyne.

Felling was remarkably unscathed as a result of the war – only five people were slightly injured compared with its near neighbour Hebburn which ended with the war with 26 deaths and 84 people injured.

To cope with food shortages and potential loss of homes due to bomb damage, a British Restaurant was set up on the High Street. This was part of a national scheme. After the war, the restaurant closed and the premises were later converted into additional shop premises for E. Walters, furnishers.

Felling Air Raid Precaution wardens, c. 1940. Councillor Jim Ancrum is pictured front row second from the right.

As with the First World War, it wasn't long before the local shops were giving their advertisements a war time 'twist'. Anticipating rationing, the Co-op were advocating the merits of registering with the Society guaranteeing they would be able to maintain food supplies. And the following year, after the blackout was in force, R. Sisterson & Son painters & decorators were advertising: '*Black outside but bright inside*' (*right*).

Between October 1939 and September 1946, the WVS made the staggering total of 16,439 sewn or knitted garments. Many of these were sent to military and naval hospitals and to bombed and homeless people and children in liberated Europe. The WVS had a clothing exchange shop on Smithburn Road.

Stuart Sisterson, who was running his father's wallpaper shop, commanded Felling's Home Guard during the war and was later promoted to command the Gateshead Battalion of the Durham Home Guard. He was given the honorary title of Lieutenant Colonel after the war ended in recognition of his service.

In 1946, a Victory Day was held when 96 children, some of whom had lost their fathers in the war, were given tea and games by the Felling British Legion women's section at St Peter's Hall. A victory cake, ice cream and sweets were all provided. In the same year the Mechanics Institute held a grand tea for 120 war widows and mothers of sons who had been killed in the war

'Last Council Meeting Ended In Uproar', 1974

Following local government reorganisation, from 1st April 1974 Felling UDC became part of Gateshead MBC. The last full Council meeting was held at Felling Council offices on 6th March 1974 but became embroiled in angry discussions. Questions were asked regarding payments for a final Felling Councillors' dinner with charges of excessive costs for this. Items mysteriously disappeared from the Agenda and the meeting finally ended, described in the local press as a '*short, hostile meeting*'.

Felling Councillors in the Council Chamber, 1966. Many of these Councillors would be at the final meetings during March 1974.

A Felling Miscellany

There have been some wonderful images of Felling people taken over the years. Sometimes, we can identify them or have details of the event at which the photograph was taken. However, often we can't but the fact that there is little if any information known about them doesn't really matter as they are such interesting pictures.

This is a mix of some identifiable and non-identifiable photographs, arranged in a roughly chronological order.

To celebrate the end of the Second Boer War in 1902, this effigy of President Kruger, the leader of the Boers, was displayed outside Sisterson's shop. The sign reads 'Lift at 10. No flowers'.

Children from Coldwell Street Primitive Methodist Sunday School, 1905.

This photograph could show celebrations at the end of the First World War but what is the jockey and his donkey doing in the photograph? Will we ever know?

Right: This may possibly show the parade which took place for the opening of the pant shown on page 36.

A lovely photograph of pit hewer James Short with his baby daughter Lydia taken in 1911, outside their home – 13 Back Dora Street.

This little group are all dressed up for a performance somewhere, probably at school – but the 'where' and 'when' remain a mystery.

Right: A group of young people in fancy dress – this could possibly be a dramatic performance probably dating to the years immediately after the First World War. This photograph was taken in the same place as the one above right showing the children dressed up.

This rather sweet image depicts the Pocock family of Felling who won first prize for their depiction of the Co-op on a float, c. 1924. From left to right: Elsie (tea), Mollie (soap), Teddy (Pelaw Polish), Jean (flour) and John (butchers).

The photograph above, taken at one of Felling's carnivals, probably dates from the 1930s. It is titled 'Off with his head'.

Four very nice young gentlemen but is this taken before a wedding perhaps or do the buttonholes symbolise something else?

'Off on a trip' – Felling Council officials and their families outside the Council office, c. 1924.

Right: Felling Church Women's Band. This is a lovely photograph – but it's a mystery. The identity of this group of ladies is unknown but their hairstyles date them to the 1930s. They are holding a variety of instruments ranging from kazoos and tambourines to a zither.